The Unnamed Algorithm

by Sarah Thursday

Table of Contents

Love Letter No.1: To My Pit-Bull Self

I love the teeth of your love
how you pit-bull deep
into the flesh of loving
How you make shrines
in the empty spaces,
abandoned apartments
Shrines to former residents
of borrowed books and toiletries
envelopes full of photographs
and letters in pen
How you never fill
the same space with new
but keep building out
expand the frames and floors
How you know when to change the locks
and when to nail it shut

I love how you calculate
estimate the risk
How you trust
the unnamed algorithm
the intuitive push, flashing *Yes,*
love this one, let that one in!
How soft your wrought-iron grip
holds every name tight
each face, its own story
each moment, a glass in your pane
How you refuse to argue
about the wrong
or right way to love

I love how so much of it matters
how you will forgive
as many times
as they will call
and ask for it
How you defend this weakness
with the expense of wasted time

Your time-to-give being
your love currency
not words, not gifts,
not your doing-for-me
But your minutes and hours
your speak to me, eat with me
your listen and watch with me
sit in this space of air
I breathe with me is love

I love how love-greedy you get
How you collect time
and stuff it in bags and boxes
shove it on shelves, in closets
covering walls, blocking doorways
in empty apartments
You guard-dog this house
an unapologetic hoarder
How you refuse to purge it
refuse to loosen your grip
Set shrines in windowsills
light blood candles
There is always room
for more

View at 4 A.M.

You, a landscape sloping
down into soft valleys
where I trace your bare
terrain outlined in moonlight
I rest on your dark side
how you speak clearest
in silence still as mountain tops
I, lying in your slant night,
an eager traveler pulling
at your dawn, sunrise us—
turn and move earth in me.

Reef of Clouds

I am a car underwater
driving through seaweed and coral
You are shark swimming
circling, circling
I have forgotten how to breathe
so I pull on blue-grey sunbeams
escalating me upwards
My lungs eat dust particles
I am phytoplankton
as small as molecules
as massive as continents
sending breath into clouds
into horizons
You are pollution
black slug of fossil fuel
I will sleep in the crook
of your arms
make you drink
in my low tide
turn you starlight

Scent-Stained

You are the mistake I want to make
I will wrap myself in your red flags
and let you peel them off
one silk layer at a time

You are the regret I want to have
I'll bind you in my caution tape
lay on a bed of warning signs
Cold metal against warm skin
cools your burning in my eyes

You are the fucked up mess
I want to roll around in
like a mud-happy dog
drenched in your scent
I will not shake you out

How do you unsense me?

Not Sleeping

I can't keep
not sleeping at night
I can't keep
letting all those
     open cupboard doors
pull my shoulder blades
I can't keep
hoping for that miracle
     change black tea
     into coffee and cream
I can't keep
recycling those words
     said and unsaid
replies and responses
never meet resolution
I can't keep
my head full of bees
whispering why
     it doesn't matter
     it never matters
I can't keep
eating the edges of my cuticles
it won't grow flat
I can't keep
my ear to my gut
it's holding on to a secret
     I'm listening
     it's not telling
I can't keep
waiting by the phone
waiting for that email
     to make it right
it will never be right
I can't keep
saying I don't mind
I get it—I understand
     I don't
I can't keep
not surrendering to anything

since the switch flipped
    it got broke
    I can't switch it back
I can't keep
a single person as ideal
as I have loved them
    stop idealizing
I can't keep
all the names off my lips
they push out daily
    hourly I form them
    my mouth aches
I can't keep
this pencil moving
    its eraser is shrinking
there's more mistakes to make
I can't keep
presuming the road's closed
my feet are swelling
    until it hurts to walk
    but I keep walking anyway
I can't keep
listening to the air in my lungs
rub against my nostrils
    I hear myself living
    I need to be sleeping

Dust Universe

When sun falls in faint slants
through holes in thin curtains
you can see the universe of dust
It hasn't traveled here
but revealed by narrow sunbeams
in the quiet light of morning
Suddenly—I am afraid to breathe
—the enormity of it
Billions of particles floating
hovering like microscopic gnats
When I see them swarming
I can't let them in my lungs
molecules of dead skin and ash
lit up as thick as stars flickering
landing in my living room
I can't tell anyone how
we are always swallowing
parts of each other
I have to keep it secret
So I open up the curtains wide
for ancient light to swallow
this exact moment in time
and deliver it to the past

The First Her

It's always dusk or dawn
in my memory. When I open my eyes,
she smiles or I see laughter in the house
though I know those days were heavy
with labor. She does laundry
in the kitchen while she cooks me eggs.
I will always eat my vegetables for her.
She always moves across this
dimly lit room. If I watch her longer,
the sun must go down. It gets
very dark for days, dark for years.
I can hear her hum, though I never
remembered her humming.
I am so small and hate to have
my hair brushed. She is every
thing that connects me
to this earth. She gives me
folded clothes to put away: my rainbow
t-shirt sparkling glitter in my hands.
Her long straight hair is perfect,
a hippie part down the middle,
always pulled back in a loose ponytail.
I remember plants in the window sills,
long green and yellow leaves.
I don't remember how
she cared for them.
She cleans other
people's houses, burns
her hands on the chemicals.
I will climb her ladders,
I will hold her razor blades
on my fingertips. No one
will notice these scars until I show them.

The First Him

It's home movies on a reel-to-reel.
Light is always dim, pouring in
from thin covered windows.
He is carpenter, framing houses.
Long days in the sun tan his skin,
make him sleep late on weekends.
We play *Ambulance* anytime I bump my head,
scrape my shin. He lifts me over his shoulders
and mocks sirens rushing hurried to hospitals.
He lays me down like a patient and makes me giggle,
fingertips under the arms, across the belly.
For seconds, I forget.
I am a laughing four-year-old unafraid.
Until I am not. Until the looming frame of him
scrapes ceilings, pulls in the weight of rooftops
down into the darkest room, windows covered thick.
He does not lock his door. I play the secret game
of *Find the place he is not.* Stay quiet enough
and he won't see you close the door.
He will not call after you.
Scratches flicker across film spliced memories
as the reel hums, tick-tick-tick-tick-tick.

Yellow

I am seven
yellow-blonde girl
with missing teeth
wearing someone else's clothes
I smile for the camera
I don't remember
where I am
there are so many rooms
so many stops
I am never there long enough
to know if I will miss it

I keep following my mother
my brother, too, in the car
we drive for days and months
I forget the names
of all my teachers
just shadows of school yards
they say I need glasses
I have too many absences
I think this is normal
don't all children hold secrets
like packs of gum
at the bottom of their pockets

I love my mother
I believe her implicitly
I walk in my sleep
in every different house
to find her
I am empty without her
so we keep our clothes in bags
and in the car
they are my sister's clothes
or someone else who outgrew them

she cuts my hair short
to get rid of the lice
it's up past my ears

I cry like a widow
yellow-blonde hair
corpses lying under my chair
I can go back to school now
the fourth one this year

twenty years later
I will return here
it will be so much smaller
the rooms will have moved
and ghosts of yellow-blonde hair
will wander in the shadows
of school yards

Child of the Alleyway

We were five, sometimes more,
in a one-bedroom duplex
with its back turned away
from the street. We made
it work, split the space

with my brother in the laundry,
and a cloth foldout couch.
We had two dogs and two cats
so the house was never empty.
I knew well the back ends

of other people's houses,
apartments and wood fences,
gardens and add-on porches.
Telephone poles like redwoods
stood in a forest of garage doors

and parking spaces, while
sunlight and shadows played
hide-and-seek across the sky.
On holidays like Thanksgiving,
food drive cans of green beans,

cranberries and yellow corn,
and boxes of instant mashed potatoes
landed on our back-front porch,
three brown steps, peeling paint
peeling wood from white washed walls.

We painted the kitchen red
with forest green trim, so
it always felt like Christmas
underneath the long wires
across much taller buildings.

White Sandals

A ten-year-old girl
stood in the alleyway

in white buckled sandals
that made her feel too tall—

like someone twelve not ten
like someone more carefree,

sandals for a girl who could just
be a girl and not—

one begging her mother not
to walk away,

pleading her only parent to stop
going farther down

into the alleyway dark.
Heels slightly wobble and tilt

on bare red ankles
on ten-year-old legs

always ready to run.

Skin As Thick As Walruses

We stopped panicking ages ago.
We take a deep breath.
One of us takes a turn
and we run the fire drill.
You want us in a crisis—
we get calmer—
we listen for the beats.
We can walk
on a turbulent plane
balancing plates and
babies on our hips.

We can direct you during disaster.
We can cover our heads,
protect our fragile necks,
and look you in the eye
while singing a peaceful song.
We know how to keep a steady hand
when cutting the wires.
We know this too shall pass.
We hum the song of the screaming siren.
We have skin as thick as walruses.

When it happens—
it   all   slows   down
the   earthquakes
the   explosions
the   car   crashes.
We do not cry—
we do not feel it—
those are luxuries
for a child born into chaos.

Those assigned to protect us
were those who sinned against us,
used us as shields, caught us
in friendly fire, or turned
and looked the other way.

We learn
hyper-vigilance,
a constant state
of preparation
for impact.
One foot ready to run
—smile at your teacher—
but keep one fist clenched
and over time it fuses
into our breath
so there are no
caught-off-guards.

No shock when your bags
are in the car before
you ever unpacked them—
no hesitation in the middle
of the night—it's time to leave—
time to keep the clothes on your back.

And your mother crying means you
make your own dinner and your
sister screaming means you keep
your eyes down—stay out of the way—
but be ready to pick out
the shrapnel— put the chairs back
on their feet—hold your breath—

don't wake the bear— don't crack
the eggs—don't make him mad— don't
cross the line— don't cry now—don't
need—don't look up— don't be
a kid— don't let your guard down—
don't flinch—don't blink—don't

We will walk through fire.
We will save your babies
and you can thank us
for pulling the earth up
on wide shoulders
or else the orbit will fail.

Fixing a Hole

How do you fill
                a chasm?
With stone or wood
                    or earth?
An artist doesn't fill
                a chasm
but instead creates
            an amphitheater
and floods the space
            with song
Steep gouged walls
become a torso
        Its beating heart
        begins to sing

Of I Ever Have Children

If I ever have children
they will never know me in my thirties
the woman checking it off
all the things-to-do
like a master's degree
and home buying
like falling in love completely
and writing a book of how it ends
finding new community
and loving her whole body flawed
flinging open all the doors
and surrendering to the unknown next

If I ever have children
they will never know me in my twenties
the woman fighting against it
to save her own soul
find her own belief in God
and lose her given self
venture out from community
live alone, love alone
sort through the old baggage
give them names and abandon them
find focus for talents and energies
and heal the damage at all costs

If I ever have children
they will never know me in my teens
young girl trying masks
on and off each year
like too many friends
and partying far too young
like black dyed-hair and boots
sinking down through the cracks
sharp turn into a Christian life
and a radical-faced community
stepping through the windows
where she'd press her face to the glass

If I ever have children
they will never know me as a child
a broken girl holding
a green Picasso heart
running with one parent from the other
always leaving school early
memories in paper bags stashed
in the trunk of a broken-down car
with walk-in closets for the skeletons
and attics for hiding and running free
words swallowed in torn pieces
forcing her destiny as a poet

January 1991

In the bathroom of that old theater
is where it started for us.
You stood by the sink
and we met eyes through the mirror.
I had cut my hair short,
dyed my blond hair black.
You were so heavy metal
with your endless platinum hair
and black suede boots with fringe
that made me resist you.
But I kept hearing rumors
that you liked my favorite bands,
like The Cure and even Scattered Few.
You were my age
and the same height as me,
we were both on the threshold
of becoming women,
of defining our future selves.
Back in nineteen ninety-one
we'd come for the same reason
to hear the bands pour their hearts out
to bare their souls on the stage.
You must have understood it
—the need to feel it raw,
the bloody heart pulsing.
I looked through the mirror at you
in that bathroom in January,
the decade still fresh and undefined.
We talked about the band
the way we always would.
You smiled with uncertainty,
I smiled back in my arrogance.

Frost

When do we lay these sticks down?
Having been rubbed raw of revival
no sparks enough for flames—
I am too tired to promise I'll wait
faithful for another dawn.
You are more in love with saving the fire
than actually keeping us
warm and free from that frost that hangs
on branches above our heads—
it's been itching at us for years.
I'm going inside the house now,
I will leave the door unlocked
but I won't leave it open.
I won't call out to you again.
My words caught in cold breath
as I pull off wet feet,
hang them on wires
stretching for decades.
Say goodbye in white crystal
particles drifting into the black.

Night Swimming as Ceremony

I didn't respect her
she was terrible at her job
we were all grateful when she was gone
it annoyed me that she wrote her name
        on the cover of my books
that none of her sets were complete
that she left a mess behind

but then   she was really gone
all those psychological stresses
were physical and actual disease

I didn't watch it happen
the last face I saw was a constant
        frantic-edge state
        dark-circled and worn
she reminded me of my mother
in her darkest times

the numb fail-safe state
I learned as a child kicks in
I feel nothing   for her

only for her children—
the ache of those young hands
the sink of those feet
the electric   quiet
left beside her husband
I can't feel the lost
        only the left

the dark placid eyes
I know as well as swimming
how ache becomes a sea
breath-holding under black skies

I'd pour out her ashes where
she left her children swimming

The Lost Vowels

They changed the spelling of my name—
too many vowels—when they crossed the ocean.
Maybe that's when France was severed from me,
my father's name simplified to the basic sounds.
It carried nothing of its history, no region or dialect,
just letters on a page that claimed I was his daughter.
Distant traces of Parisian ancestry,
to layers of circling city streets and rolling country hills,
to some thick summer air lingering
across vineyards and farmlands,
I've felt nothing for her.
As if vowels lost were codes in my DNA
spliced by some genetic scientist
leaving me a stranger to my own name.
I've never felt those ancestral threads
pulling me back in time, discover the land
of a name that never existed on its soil.
I have no love for my paternity.
Even through a Canadian migration,
through a western reach and down to California,
there is no curiosity in her truth.
I write only five letters of my American name,
five letters I have defined and redefined
a thousand times and again.
I know more of Mexico—my neighbor
who has fed me my whole life.
I know more of Long Beach—its long avenues
and dimly lit streets. I know more
of California—not the one on TV—
but the long Pacific Coast, the cliffs of Highway 101,
the endless sky of the 5 and its pink dawn
across thousands of farmlands and
hundreds of thick summer nights,
the progression of her cities, young but in love
with all of us—rich and poor,
the Britneys and the Caesars, the Tyrones
and the Isabellas, the been-theres and the dreamers.
She is my sister and my ancestor,
we create our own motherland. I've never
been lost to her once.

Unnamed

Write about important things
things that move me
things that crush me

Write about hurricanes
and avalanches
the earthquakes of my soul

It's the grit beneath
my fingernails
it's the cartilage in
my vertebrae

I am driven to expose it
to pull it out
hold it up
to the light

I am only the messenger
of all the beauty
underneath the common face
beauty in the unheard voice

I hear it
I draw the letters
to form the words
to give it name

My Friends Who Write Poetry

Our words swing from threads
across our chest. They pull,
unraveling thin lines into
a soft jagged mess.
Some of you fight it,
snip those frays clean,
tuck in all the evidence.
Some dig fingers deep
wearing fringe coats
long into summer nights.
I know a poet when I see
your words dangling,
dragging, spilling like
sloppy rainbows
out from our pockets.

About the Author

Sarah Thursday is a local Long Beach poetry advocate, editor of CadenceCollective.net, founder of Sadie Girl Press and cofounder of Lucid Moose Lit. She has happily merged her favorite things (poetry, music, art, and friends) in collaborative projects and events. Co-hosting 2nd Mondays Poetry Party with G. Murray Thomas and having countless poetry adventures with Nancy Lynée Woo have been her most cherished memories of 2014. If you must know what means most to her in her poetry world, it's when one of her poems stays with someone or if someone has been inspired to start writing poetry of their own. (Photo by Mick Victor)

Acknowledgements

Thank you to the following publications where each of the poems in this book were published in 2014:

The Bastille
Cadence Collective
Cliterature: Climax Issue
Disorder: Mental Illness and Its Affects
East Jasmine Review
Elsewhere Lit
Ishaan Lit Review
The Mayo Review
The Rainbow Journal
San Gabriel Valley Poetry Quarterly
Self Portrait Series Collection (Silver Birch Press)
Something's Brewing (Kind of a Hurricane Press)
Uno Kudo Literary & Arts Magazine

Thank you, my incredible community of poets, musicians, and artists who I am very fortunate to know. Nancy, Murray, Raquel, JL, Mickie, Terrianne, Fernando, Aly, Terry, Elmast, Esmeralda, Sean, and my loving family of misfits. Let's make more magic together!

www.ingramcontent.com/pod-product-compliance
Lightning Source LLC
Chambersburg PA
CBHW051742040426
42447CB00008B/1264